Change Your Own Diaper

Katey

Hope this makes you laugh out loud!

6·8·23

Change Your Own Diaper

A Bachelor with No Kids Explains
How to Be a Parent without Screwing Up

NICK KRAUTTER

REAL ESTATE BUSINESS PRESS

Line editing, proofreading, cover design, and interior book design provided by Indigo: Editing, Design, and More:

- Line editor: Kristen Hall-Geisler
- Proofreaders: Sarah Currin and Bailey Potter
- Book designer: Vinnie Kinsella

www.indigoediting.com

Paperback ISBN: 978-0-9968146-4-5
Hardback ISBN: 978-0-9968146-6-9
Ebook ISBN: 978-0-9968146-5-2

This book is dedicated to my parents, who managed to raise me and my little brother into well-adapted and successful adults. This is despite the fact that we moved into a tent in the middle of the woods filled with wild animals for a summer before they made us help build a house (possibly violating child labor laws). We were also tricked into getting good grades and playing sports every single season. On the plus side, we got to have BB gun fights, build unpermitted tree houses, and camp and fish in the wilds of Northern California.

Contents

Disclaimer

This is not a real book.

Well, the book itself is a real book, but all the advice in it is completely made up and has no scientific merit whatsoever. This book is a satire, so for god's sake, please don't actually do anything it recommends. If you are offended by anything in the book, please call all local media outlets and city councils and make sure to get the book banned in your area.

Picking a Favorite

I know that each of your kids is special and wonderful, but let's be honest: One of them is clearly smarter and loves to follow the rules and get your approval. You started looking into trade schools for one of your kids around third grade. Then there's the kid who never listens and has been throwing a sixteen-year-long tantrum. You can't give each kid the same time and attention, so here's how to #PickAFavorite.

Real Job

Step 1: Give your kids chores.
Step 2: Whoever gets the chores done is your favorite.

HELPFUL HINTS! Kids are expensive, so see if the neighbors have chores and charge $10 an hour per kid under the table.

Fancy Job

Step 1: Give your kids an allowance.
Step 2: Track who saves the most money.
Step 3: The kid who saves the most will be the most likely to care for you in old age, so they are your favorite.

HELPFUL HINTS! Give your kids a big enough allowance to cover their clothes and let them shop on their own. Think of all the time you'll save!

Trust Fund

Step 1: Create a series of physical and mental challenges.
Step 2: Take the top two kids from Step 1 and give them each $100,000.
Step 3: See who uses the $100,000 best to win political favor and positive PR for one of your ventures. This kid will be the most likely to take over your empire.

HELPFUL HINTS! Use the margin account at your brokerage to borrow the $200,000 at below retail interest.

How to Build a Crib
without Getting Divorced

Y ou are about to buy a ton of stuff you never thought you'd own, and that includes a crib. A crib is a #BabyPrison that will allow you a couple hours of peace. Like many complicated household projects, building a crib can sometimes lead to divorce. Here's how to defend your union and keep the peace while you build a crib.

Real Job

Step 1: Let her pick out the crib.
Step 2: Assemble it in the garage.
Step 3: Redo it since you didn't read the directions.

HELPFUL HINTS! Make sure you hide enough beer in the garage.

Fancy Job

Step 1: Have your assistant send your wife some options and schedule home assembly.
Step 2: Add the crib-building date to your shared calendar.
Step 3: Post some pics to your socials and celebrate the milestone with a nice chardonnay.

HELPFUL HINTS! Chill the wine two hours before your date. Make sure to be supportive and present.

Trust Fund

Step 1: Acknowledge that your furniture is a reflection of your character and values.
Step 2: Pick a style that fits your baby's identity.
Step 3: Choose a sustainably harvested exotic hardwood.

HELPFUL HINTS! Have your attorney trademark your new crib design. Have your PR rep get you a feature in *Fine Woodworking*.

Everyone Gets a Trophy

They say that 90 percent of success is showing up, but let's be honest: most kids are losers, and we all know it. When you take part in a sport or competition, there are winners and losers. In many competitions there are the top three places and then everyone else. At some point someone decided that everyone gets a trophy. Here's how to pretend your kid won when they didn't or explain to your awesome winner kid why everyone is getting the same trophy even though they are clearly the MVP. It's not fair, but #EveryoneGetsATrophy.

Real Job

Step 1: First-, second-, and third-place trophies go on the mantel.
Step 2: Participation trophies go in a box in the garage.

HELPFUL HINTS! Explain to your kid that life isn't fair, and if you don't win, you didn't win, and the only prize is more practice.

Fancy Job

Step 1: Remember that your kid is in a sport this season.
Step 2: Talk about the importance of third-grade soccer to the development of a winner's attitude.

HELPFUL HINTS! All trophies are celebrated, and the prize is soccer camp later this season.

Trust Fund

Step 1: Have your assistant find the best coach for each sport.
Step 2: Take time to ensure your kid knows that winning is the only thing that matters.
Step 3: Consult with your family doctor and attorney on the pros and cons of teen steroid use.

HELPFUL HINTS! Have your family therapist tell your kid that participation trophies are symbols of a lack of preparation and the desire to win.

Stupid Questions

Anyone who believes there's no such thing as stupid questions probably hasn't managed a discount retail store. There are tons of stupid questions in life such as: Why am I here? Is there a god? What is my purpose? How do I cancel this charge for a T-shirt I accidentally scanned twice? Etc., etc., etc. You don't want people to laugh at your kid, so here's my guide to avoiding #StupidQuestions.

Real Job

Step 1: Have your kid help you replace a broken ceiling fan.
Step 2: Ask, "Should we turn off the breaker first?"

HELPFUL HINTS! Stupid question! The fan is on a switch, and as long as it's off, there's no power to the fixture.

Fancy Job

Step 1: Have your kid help you schedule an electrician to replace a broken ceiling fan.
Step 2: Ask, "Should we get more than one bid before we pick an electrician?"

HELPFUL HINTS! Stupid question! It will cost you more in lost time, even if the first electrician is gouging you.

Trust Fund

Step 1: Apparently there is a broken ceiling fan.
Step 2: Ask, "What's the most cost-efficient way to replace a broken fixture?"

HELPFUL HINTS! Stupid question! If it's that hot, you should just go to the lake house and let the property manager deal with it.

Family Road Trip!

There's nothing more American than a road trip. Road trips are better than baseball, apple pie, and hot-dog-eating contests combined. I have great news: there are holidays and events throughout the year that almost *require* you to go on a road trip. So pack your bags, fill a grocery bag with snacks, and get ready to have the best #FamilyRoadTrip ever!

Real Job

Step 1: Either get there in three hours or find a cool place to stop in the middle.

Step 2: Did everyone go to the bathroom?

HELPFUL HINTS! If you know you'll have to stop every hour, you won't be as upset when it happens.

Fancy Job

Step 1: Pack one of those flip-card games where you ask questions and get to know each other better.

Step 2: Did everyone go to the bathroom?

HELPFUL HINTS! Make sure you have a good podcast downloaded for when the kids refuse to play the ask-and-answer-questions game for three hours.

Trust Fund

Step 1: Make sure no one brings smelly food on the jet.

Step 2: Did everyone go to the bathroom?

HELPFUL HINTS! There's really no point driving somewhere unless it's less than three hours away.

Selling Your Kids
on the Benefits of Bedtime

Eighty-seven percent of parenting is a decades-long negotiation pitting your grown-up wisdom against the tyrannical whims of your child. What makes this negotiation so difficult is that as a parent you have no solid BATNA (best alternative to a negotiated agreement). So instead of thinking of this as a negotiation, think of it as a sales pitch. Your mission, if you choose to accept it, is to #SellYourKidsOnBedtime.

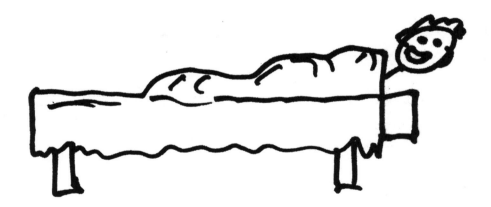

Real Job

Step 1: If you're awake, you're doing chores or homework.
Step 2: Bedtime isn't so bad after all.

HELPFUL HINTS! If your kids can sleep in until 8:00 a.m. on the weekends, they can have chocolate for breakfast.

Fancy Job

Step 1: If you're awake, you're practicing Mandarin.
Step 2: Bedtime isn't so bad after all.

HELPFUL HINTS! Try a bedtime story about the wonderful dreams that only happen when you're sleeping.

Trust Fund

Step 1: If you're awake, you're practicing negotiation tactics.
Step 2: The kids aren't the only ones with Adderall—we can do this *all night*!

HELPFUL HINTS! You can use a reverse auction technique and wake them up to practice negotiation. They'll get so tired of it, you won't need to sell bedtime ever again!

Summer Camp

Some of the most memorable moments of my youth happened at summer camp. I remember being scared of what would happen after being dropped off at a dusty meadow in the woods surrounded by a bunch of old cabins. I remember shooting bows and arrows, going on hikes, canoeing around a lake (which was most likely just a large pond), and having probably the best and most inconvenient boner of my life slow dancing to Richard Marx's "Endless Summer Nights" under café lights and the stars in the Sierra Nevada mountains. Here's how to find a great camp for your kids and get a much-needed week off from #EndlessParenting.

Real Job

Step 1: Convince your kids that camp is kid vacation.
Step 2: Get them to do extra chores for the neighbors to raise money for their "tuition."

HELPFUL HINTS! Pick a camp that's far enough away that if they get sick or sprain an ankle, you can't get time off work to pick them up. Take the week off work and have your own vacation.

Fancy Job

Step 1: Does anyone need to learn to shoot a bow and arrow anymore?
Step 2: The best lesson is being grateful for how good you have it in life.

HELPFUL HINTS! Sign your kids up to volunteer at a nature camp for kids from urban areas and save the money you would have wasted on band camp. No one plays a clarinet after high school anyway.

Trust Fund

Step 1: Your kids are already in a boarding school.
Step 2: Make sure the boarding school has a camp as well.

HELPFUL HINTS! You don't want the kids home all summer. The yacht doesn't have unlimited bunks, after all.

How to Beat Your Kid at Sports

Sports are the best way to teach your kid about real life. In real life there are winners and losers, resources are not unlimited, and there are no trophies just for showing up. Sports teach work ethic, camaraderie, focus, and desire. I grew up in a small town, and when I was a kid and the high school football team lost, I would cry. When I was on that team in high school and we lost, we would cry. Not because we were wimps, but because we cared about winning and not letting our teammates and our town down. It's important that your kid respects you, and the best way to do that is to dominate them at any and every sport you play together. Here's how to #BeatYourKidAtSports.

Real Job

Step 1: Fishing is a sport.

Step 2: At high school graduation, teach your kid about the lures they should have been using for the last fourteen years instead of the useless lures you've been giving them.

HELPFUL HINTS! If you notice your kid has one of the real lures, you can de-barb it with some needle-nose pliers when they're not looking.

Fancy Job

Step 1: Racquetball is a sport.

Step 2: Loosen the strings on your kid's racket.

HELPFUL HINTS! When your kid gets better and you're on the brink of losing, you can fake a cramp.

Trust Fund

Step 1: Polo is a sport.

Step 2: Pop-Pop gets the fastest horses.

HELPFUL HINTS! My favorite thing about polo is that the horse has to do all the running. You can beat your kid with a faster horse, accurate passing, and shots on goal. If your kid breaks away, just hook them before they score.

Trick or Treat!

I'm pretty sure the first ten years of my life were just a series of pranks my parents played on me. Nowhere is this more evident than Halloween, when my mom dressed me up in the most ridiculous costumes possible. The worst one was as an electrical outlet that was drawn on a dishwasher box that I had to walk around in all day. An electrical outlet—who even thinks of that?! The second-worst childhood costume was a cherry tomato. Seriously?! Now that you're a parent, you get to relive those precious childhood moments—and whether that means trick or treat is up to you. Happy Halloween!

Real Job

Step 1: Find some old sheets.
Step 2: Everyone is a ghost until they're at least six.

HELPFUL HINTS! Make sure you don't cut holes in the new sheets, or you'll be using them to make your bed on the couch. The one in the garage.

Fancy Job

Step 1: Have a family meeting about cultural appropriation.
Step 2: Nothing your kids want to wear is unoffensive. Everyone is a ghost.

HELPFUL HINTS! Make sure to use organic cotton sheets.

Trust Fund

Step 1: Let your kids pick whatever they want.
Step 2: Leave them with the staff and fly to Key West.

HELPFUL HINTS! When you find out your kids picked the most offensive costumes possible, make sure to delete the photos and keep them off social media. You don't want that to come back to haunt you when one of them is prime minister, eh?

Successful Holiday Photos

Congratulations! You've almost made it to the end of another year, and as a reward you get to send everyone a holiday photo of your family. Each year I love getting photos from family and friends of their little tribes. Some are just montages of that year's highlights, some are themed, some have long letters included that make you feel guilty about not reading said letters. We all know having kids is mostly about trying to impress your friends, so here's how to take #SuccessfulHolidayPhotos.

Real Job

Step 1: Everyone gets a haircut.
Step 2: Wear nice clothes.

HELPFUL HINTS! Get the dog a fresh blaze orange collar so he doesn't look shabby this year.

Fancy Job

Step 1: Everyone gets a haircut.
Step 2: Pick a theme, but not one that appropriates any cultural stereotypes.

HELPFUL HINTS! Yes, you can do *Back to the Future* again this year. Your mom is the only person who saved the card from four years ago.

Trust Fund

Step 1: Have your assistant schedule the stylist to come to the house so everyone can get a haircut.
Step 2: Plan some time for damage control when your wife realizes she wore Prada last year and can't possibly wear a dress from last season for something as important as the family holiday photo.

HELPFUL HINTS! Don't forget the Xanax and champagne.

Kid Divorce:
Late-Stage Adoption for Teens

L et's face it. Sometimes things just don't work out. People get divorced all the time, right? And that divorce comes after you had the chance to pick your mate and spend time together as adults before you decided to get married. No one knows what they're getting when they have a kid, so what's so shameful about deciding to adopt out your kid when they're in their teens? Here's my easy guide to #KidDivorce.

Real Job

Step 1: Your kid is being a real pain.
Step 2: Army or Navy?

HELPFUL HINTS! It's surprisingly easy to change the date on that birth certificate so your fifteen-year-old can enlist now and skip the wait.

Fancy Job

Step 1: Your kid is being a real pain.
Step 2: Who knew emancipation was so easy in your state?

HELPFUL HINTS! Kids think they're the only ones who can forge a signature. So cute. Now you can file for emancipation online.

Trust Fund

Step 1: Your kid is being a real pain.
Step 2: Send them to work at your fabric mill in India.

HELPFUL HINTS! Use a student visa to ship your kid to India and have your nanny complete an online course in your kid's name.

How to Worry about Concussions

Modern life is incredibly dangerous. I'm kidding; it's so hard to die that most people die of eating too much. In the early days of humankind, people would die from minor infections, get hacked up in battle with dull swords and axes, and dysentery (like in *The Oregon Trail*, the video game where you used an actual floppy disk in a computer that was slower than your Wi-Fi-connected microwave). But now life is safe, warm, and organic. So here's how to worry about concussions.

Real Job

Step 1: Make sure your kid's helmet fits tight.
Step 2: Don't forget to bring your flask to the Friday night game.

HELPFUL HINTS! Remember when this game was about hard defense?

Fancy Job

Step 1: Is soccer really safer than football?
Step 2: Make your kid wear headgear if they want to head the ball.

HELPFUL HINTS! Make sure to check for concussions when they get beat up after the game for wearing headgear.

Trust Fund

Step 1: There are no life lessons that can't be learned in the boxing ring.
Step 2: Why do you need headgear if you're wearing gloves?

HELPFUL HINTS! Ok, so maybe the headgear isn't a bad idea—you'd hate to ruin that aristocratic nose.

Sharing

Everything in life worth having is better when you share. Imagine having a private island and no one to hang out with—talk about missing the point! There's a reason why cars have at least two seats, so if life is a journey, then it's definitely a trip that is more fun when shared. The problem is that our reptilian brain constantly worries about running out of food and makes us want to hoard resources. Here's how to fight biology and teach #Sharing.

Real Job

Step 1: Buy your kid a football.
Step 2: You can't play catch alone.

HELPFUL HINTS! Make sure to convince your kid that being a receiver is cooler than being QB or you'll have to run around the whole time.

Fancy Job

Step 1: Buy your kid a soccer ball.
Step 2: You can't play soccer alone.

HELPFUL HINTS! Teach your kid an abundance-based mindset and convince them to give away their soccer ball at the end of the season. Then let them pick out a new one.

Trust Fund

Step 1: Buy your kid a sailboat.
Step 2: You can't race alone.

HELPFUL HINTS! Teach your kid how to tack as close to the wind as possible. There's nothing sweeter to share than the trophy for the summer series at the yacht club!

No, You Can't Get a Puppy: Preparing Your Kid for a Lifetime of Disappointment

No matter how much money and power you have, disappointment will visit you many times in life. Humans have an amazing ability to adapt to life circumstances both good and bad. The difference between winners and losers in life is the ability to face disappointment and still get up and try again. These days most parents make the huge mistake of trying to make life perfect for their kids. If you want to give your kids a chance at success in life, make sure they are disappointed on a regular basis. You don't get to be a hero without a journey filled with obstacles and setbacks.

Real Job

Step 1: Your kid will ask for a puppy.
Step 2: Tell them they can't get a puppy.

HELPFUL HINTS! Ask a neighbor with a grumpy, senile dog if your kids can play with it sometimes. The dog will probably just sleep a lot, and your kids will lose interest.

Fancy Job

Step 1: Your kid will ask for a puppy.
Step 2: Explain that your schedule doesn't allow for responsibilities like a puppy.

HELPFUL HINTS! Take them to volunteer day at the pound. You'll get the day off work for a volunteer day, and your kid will get to play with puppies. Get one of those weird Japanese robot dogs; it's almost like the real thing, without all the walking or emotional bonding.

Trust Fund

Step 1: Tell your kid they can have a puppy if they can turn a profit in the next twelve months.
Step 2: If they hit the goal, change the rules.
Step 3: Explain that this is the difference between being head of sales and being the owner of the company.

HELPFUL HINTS! Nothing ruins a family legacy like kids who never make an effort out of laziness or a fear of failure. Reward your kid for taking on big risks and big goals. Each time they fail, they grow and get closer to winning. Build a fire inside so they don't waste their lives trying to impress people at cheesy dance clubs.

No Meltdowns

Kids are like little nuclear power plants: when something goes wrong, alarms blare and demand attention. Unlike nuclear power, which is supposed to work forever, kids typically last two hours after a meal before their cute eyes start to water and their face scrunches up and you know your night with friends is about to end. Yet there is a secret method I've developed and tested over the years with my friend's kids called "no meltdowns." You look at the kid seriously, like they're a new hire, and simply say, "No meltdowns." Trust me, kids know what it means when you say #NoMeltdowns.

Real Job

Step 1: Calmly explain that meltdowns equal bedtime.
Step 2: By the time your kid is four, this will start working.

HELPFUL HINTS! If your kid is crying, hand him back to his mommy. Mommies can fix anything.

Fancy Job

Step 1: The first parenting book you read said to comfort your kid in melt-down.
Step 2: The second parenting book you read said to let your kid in meltdown self-soothe.

HELPFUL HINTS! Please just try the stupid "no meltdowns" trick a couple times.

Trust Fund

Step 1: You notice your kid starting to melt down.
Step 2: Tell them, "No meltdowns."

HELPFUL HINTS! If they still melt down (unlikely!), hand them to one of your nannies and have them sent to the opposite wing of the house.

Because I Said So:
Reasons Are for Wimps

There are very few times in life when you are a god and a slave at the same time. As a parent you are a slave to the responsibilities of constant care and feeding of your helpless baby. But there is a plus side to being a #BabySlave since you are also an all-powerful #ParentGod. As a god you can provide and take away whatever you choose. Just remember that no one gets to question God's wrath or charity. Take a cue from God and don't explain yourself; reasons are for wimps.

Real Job

Step 1: Your kid refuses to eat their vegetables.
Step 2: Tell them they have to because you said so.

HELPFUL HINTS! Don't give in to the temptation to negotiate or just give up out of exhaustion. Be strong—you're the boss now!

Fancy Job

Step 1: Your kid refuses to eat their vegetables.
Step 2: Tell them they have to because you said so.

HELPFUL HINTS! You remember a technique from a parenting book (a real one) and start to explain the benefits of vegetables. Your kid has no idea what you're talking about.

Trust Fund

Step 1: Your kid refuses to eat their vegetables.
Step 2: Tell them they have to because you said so.

HELPFUL HINTS! You remember a reverse auction technique you used when your REIT (real estate investment trust) was buying distressed assets. Every time your kid refuses to eat vegetables, you give them more vegetables. You smile because you know you will win.

Aggressive Driving for Teens

Remember back in high school when they taught defensive driving? It was mostly based on going slow, having enough buffer space between you and the car in front of you, and signaling a turn three blocks before you actually needed to turn. What a shame to waste that youthful split-second reaction time on driving like a grandpa. They're not putting 400-horsepower engines in every modern car so you can drive the speed limit, and your teen will not be driving slowly. Here's how to teach #AggressiveDriving.

Real Job

Step 1: Your kid gets to drive an old truck with a three-speed and drum brakes.
Step 2: It does 0–60 mph in 12 seconds.

HELPFUL HINTS! There's nothing more fun than peeling out on a gravel road. Even if they crash, you just pull the truck back out of the ditch and hammer out the dents.

Fancy Job

Step 1: If your kid makes the dean's list, they get to go to racing school.
Step 2: Sign yourself up for racing school too.

HELPFUL HINTS! Spend the weekend trying to outrace your kid, then remind them that racing is just for the track — wink, wink.

Trust Fund

Step 1: A BMW M3 seems like a reasonable sixteenth birthday present.
Step 2: Have one of the drivers from your F1 team teach your kid to drive.

HELPFUL HINTS! Put the family attorney's and private mechanic's phone numbers on the dash of the car. If they crash the M3, they get a Volvo wagon for their next car.

Socializing Your Kid

A well-liked idiot will go further and have a better life than a smart jerk. With that in mind, your number-one goal in life is to make sure you socialize your kid to get along with others. This will take a mix of having enough empathy to be likable and enough competitive spirit to still win (most of the time). Don't feel like you have to do all the work, though. School, slumber parties, summer camps, and sports teams are all available and ready to help make your ornery kid a social genius. The other good news is that you get roughly eighteen years to work on #SocializingYourKid.

Real Job

Step 1: Summer break is for kids, and you're working two jobs.
Step 2: Team sports every season.

HELPFUL HINTS! Your dad didn't go to every game you played and you still made state!

Fancy Job

Step 1: It's important to think about college as soon as possible.
Step 2: Craft a calendar of volunteer, sporting, and learning camps so your kid can work with all types of people and situations.

HELPFUL HINTS! You'll know you've won if your kids can have fun with other kids and hold a decent conversation with adults by no later than age five.

Trust Fund

Step 1: Normal kids are easy to get along with.
Step 2: Focus your socializing efforts on how to navigate the choppy waters of the rich and insecure.

HELPFUL HINTS! Have your kids read *The 48 Laws of Power*, but not too soon or they'll use that knowledge against you.

Screen Time Strategies

Like all new parents, you want the best for your kids. You've read the studies that say too much screen time is warping the impressionable minds of today's youth. But eventually you'll get exhausted and give up. Just like the story of the tree falling in the woods, is it too much screen time if no one outside the family knows about it? Below are some strategies for #ScreenTime.

Real Job

Step 1: If the kids do their chores, they get one hour a day with the Fire tablet.

Step 2: If the kids don't do their chores, hide the charger until they get back in line.

HELPFUL HINTS! You can double up snuggle time and your favorite show together after the kids go to sleep.

Fancy Job

Step 1: If the kids maintain a 3.75 GPA, they get the iPad Pro for non-school work for an hour.

Step 2: For every hour they spend on a foreign language app, they get thirty more minutes of screen time.

HELPFUL HINTS! Wait! Some kid won three million dollars playing Fortnight? Unlimited screen time if they can stay in the top five.

Trust Fund

Step 1: Your PR people convince you an RV trip with the family will make you appear more down to earth and likable.

Step 2: After the first hour, you let the kids watch unlimited cartoons so they stop fighting.

HELPFUL HINTS! What's more down to earth and likable than a family fighting on a road trip? The TV viewers eat up the "just like us" segment and photo series in *People*.

Advice for Single Dads

L ife doesn't always turn out like you plan. Your marriage started out as a blissful couple of years of travel, sex, and dinner parties. Pretty soon kids come into the picture, and your golf game goes to hell. At the beginning you were too irresponsible, but now you work too much and aren't present enough. Once the kids start school, your wife might start to wonder if she needs you around at all anymore. But if you can't even agree on what kind of ketchup to buy, don't despair; here's my advice for #SingleDads.

Real Job

Step 1: This is a choose-your-own-adventure story.

Step 2: If you have the kids, immediately marry your backup lady from church—you know, the one who's always asking if she can help with the kids and has secretly been in love with you.

Step 3: If you don't have the kids, immediately start dating younger women and go fishing four days a week.

HELPFUL HINTS! If you're coparenting, you'll have to compromise eventually.

Fancy Job

Step 1: Set up your dating app profile(s) with the help of a single friend.

Step 2: Set your target age range between twenty-five and fifty.

HELPFUL HINTS! Make sure to get some advice from your single friends. It's a crazy world out there, and you've been out of the game for a decade.

Trust Fund

Step 1: Hire a night nanny.

Step 2: Everyone at the athletic club already knows you're single.

HELPFUL HINTS! Be discreet. The ladies will want to lay claim to you, so stay away from the Instagram models who overshare.

Advice for Single Moms

Life doesn't always turn out like you plan. Maybe you decided to have a kid on your own because you didn't want to settle for some average guy. Maybe you married that average guy and the towering resentment finally killed your union. Or maybe that average guy left you when the reality of being a parent set in, and he chickened out. Don't despair—there are some great upsides to this life. Here's advice for being a #SingleMom.

Real Job

Step 1: Have your mom move in with you to help with the kids.
Step 2: Finally finish that dental assistant program you had to quit when you got pregnant.

HELPFUL HINTS! Make sure you get a job with a dentist that is either single or unhappily married. You'll be in a gated community by the end of the year.

Fancy Job

Step 1: Make sure you dictate the coparenting schedule.
Step 2: Exercise four times a week and party like you're twenty-two whenever you don't have the kids.

HELPFUL HINTS! Eventually you'll realize that only another single parent will take a future together seriously, but until then, the world is full of young, athletic guys with something to prove, and your body has never looked better.

Trust Fund

Step 1: Reconnect with an eccentric surfer artist your ex bought a collection from.
Step 2: Have a very public affair on social media.

HELPFUL HINTS! That collection will quadruple in value, but your ex will sell it now anyway out of sheer frustration.

Yes, You Can Be a Billionaire: Accepting That Your Kids Will Do More than You

Every parent hopes their kids will have a better life than they've had—until it actually happens and your twenty-eight-year-old millionaire kid starts explaining how you should live *your* life. What the hell do they know, anyway?! They don't know how hard you had it when you were their age. Have they forgotten how many advantages you gave them in life? Take a deep breath and try to keep it in perspective. The alternative to accepting that your kids will do more than you is having them move back home and work on a screenplay for the next three years.

Real Job

Step 1: Your kid will get a job in sales.
Step 2: They make more than you, and they just turned twenty-three.

HELPFUL HINTS! Convince them to buy your fishing boat and store it at your house. Use it the same amount as you always have.

Fancy Job

Step 1: Help your kid get a summer internship at your firm.
Step 2: Your kid will land a huge client through their fraternity connections and get promoted in their first year.

HELPFUL HINTS! You are so happy and proud of your kid—until you realize they might be your boss in two years. Move to a new firm.

Trust Fund

Step 1: Your kid's first company just had an IPO with a valuation of $500 million.
Step 2: Buy her biggest competitor and give her a run for her money.

HELPFUL HINTS! You have no idea what the competitor you just bought actually does. Hire your nephew to run the company and task him to double revenue in two years. Eventually buy your kid's company in a hostile takeover.

How to Bond with Your Kid
without Wasting All That Time

The best and worst part of raising kids is the first couple years, when they can't even talk or hold a decent conversation. You grind your teeth when you think of all the time and money and sleep you've lost to make a kid, and then they're pretty boring for the first couple years. But hang in there, because soon your kid will be talking—and then talking back. It's critical that you bond with your kid so they will feel obligated to take care of you when you're old. Life is short, so here's how to bond without wasting all that time.

Real Job

Step 1: Now that you have three kids, you can finally build your dream home with free labor.

Step 2: Nothing will help you bond more than hammering some nails at 5:00 a.m. sharp.

HELPFUL HINTS! Carhartt makes kids' clothes for a reason. First kid to wear a hole through their pants gets a new bike!

Fancy Job

Step 1: It's difficult to tell the difference between fear and love.

Step 2: Take your kids canoeing at Lake Louise (known for its icy blue water) and jokingly rock the boat.

HELPFUL HINTS! Some of my favorite memories are of canoeing with my family; I even fell in once. Memory for life!

Trust Fund

Step 1: Have your assistant schedule time to take the kids out of boarding school.

Step 2: Have a list of questions prepared.

HELPFUL HINTS! Take them on your flight from NYC to London. Five hours is plenty of time to talk about the last semester and properly bond for this quarter.

Getting into the Best School

College isn't for everyone. Even *Time* magazine recently questioned if spending the money it takes to get through college is worth the cost anymore. Let's be real, though: No one in their teens knows who they want to be, and college is a great place to send them, unless you want them to join the military. So if your kids are going to college, make sure they get into the best one they can. Or if you have the money, send your kids to any school you want, even if they aren't that special. I mean, most Ivy League school endowments are dangerously low right now, right?

Real Job

Step 1: Fancy universities are a luxury that put you more in debt than a mortgage.

Step 2: Get your kid into a trade school, and they can go to community college on their own dime if they want.

HELPFUL HINTS! Have you hired an electrician or plumber lately? I know attorneys who make less per hour, and your kid will get an eight-year head start on their career.

Fancy Job

Step 1: Get your daughter golf lessons starting at age five.

Step 2: If she can shoot par golf in tournaments, she can punch her own ticket anywhere.

HELPFUL HINTS! Make sure she does some volunteer work between the four hours of practice and eight hours of school and homework per day. Colleges love that stuff.

Trust Fund

Step 1: Your family is legacy at two competing Ivy League colleges.

Step 2: Make the colleges compete for your kid's attendance and your "continued support."

HELPFUL HINTS! Your kid's network of friends from either school will set them up for a life of success (and excess). Make sure they can letter in at least one sport; life is about being well rounded, right?

There's Always the Military

Most countries have a long tradition of military service. Some countries even make service mandatory for its citizens. The military can be a great option if going to college, trade school, or doing nothing aren't options. There are even military schools for youths who need a little more structure and guidance in life. Here's how to start dropping hints to your kids that the military is way better than living at home in their twenties.

Real Job

Step 1: You just spent eighteen years raising your kid.
Step 2: Make it clear they will be leaving the nest one way or another.

HELPFUL HINTS! You've shared your stories of Fleet Week, so the Navy should be a lock.

Fancy Job

Step 1: It's clear your kid will not make it through their first semester at their current maturity level.
Step 2: Think of the money the GI bill will save you since you underfunded that college savings account!

HELPFUL HINTS! The Coast Guard counts as the military, right?

Trust Fund

Step 1: The eldest son has attended West Point for the last four generations.
Step 2: You're still angry that your older brother got to go while you studied financial models at Yale.

HELPFUL HINTS! Football or fencing team? Can't you do both?

The Birds and the Bees

I love nature shows, but I'm pretty sure I've never seen a bird mate with a bee. Like many other metaphors that don't really make sense, let's just jump in the pool and have the most awkward conversation of your lifetime. The good news is that because the internet is raising our kids these days, they probably know more about sex than you do. This is your chance to set the record straight on love, sex, disease, and pregnancy—just what every thirteen-year-old is dying to talk about with their parents.

Real Job

Step 1: Convince your kids they will get pregnant and catch an STD the first time they have sex.

Step 2: Recall that the church's abstinence program worked great for half of the kids in your high school.

HELPFUL HINTS! If you remember all the trouble you got into in school, you know you're going to just have to have "the talk." Your kid will be more embarrassed than you, and that should make you feel better.

Fancy Job

Step 1: You know that love and sex are integral parts of a successful and happy life.

Step 2: Talk with your kid like an adult about the pros and cons of sex and risk.

HELPFUL HINTS! If you talk with your kids about sex in a practical way, there will be no taboo about it, and they'll probably wait until college just so they don't have to talk with you about it ever again.

Trust Fund

Step 1: You make sure to spend quality time with your kids a couple holidays a year.

Step 2: Confirm that your nanny and boarding school are explaining this stuff to your kid.

HELPFUL HINTS! The real goal is to make sure your daughter doesn't make a sex tape that gets "leaked" to launch her modeling career.

How to Give Up and Embrace the Chaos

Remember when you knew where your keys were and there weren't Legos in every room? Remember sleeping in on a lazy Saturday? Those days are long gone now. But don't despair: one of the gifts of parenting is a complete reprioritizing of what constitutes a real problem and what is just the static hum of a family household. House always messy? No problem. Snot and spit on all your clothes? No problem. You both think the other parent is picking up the kids from camp? Actual problem.

Real Job

Step 1: Your kids leave toys all over the place.
Step 2: Start hiding the toys in the garage and go play with them yourself.

HELPFUL HINTS! Invent an #AntiSanta that steals toys that are left out after bedtime. Regift those toys at Christmas.

Fancy Job

Step 1: Your kid fingerpainted the living room wall while you were taking a shower.
Step 2: Hang up canvases on the wall for your kid to paint and sell them online.

HELPFUL HINTS! The art world is obsessed with youth. Position your child as an art genius, and maybe you can use that college fund for a yacht once they get a full ride.

Trust Fund

Step 1: Junior just threw up in the Bentley.
Step 2: Immediately have it detailed.

HELPFUL HINTS! Install an absorbent blanket around every child seat in your cars. Bentley makes an SUV now, much more practical than the sedan.

Slumber Party of the Year!

Our lives are mostly made of boring and forgettable years punctuated by small dashes of brilliant moments. These moments are what we will remember in the end: brilliant moments like your first kiss, falling in love, your first car crash, and the winning catch. Part of your job as a parent is to create these memories for your family. What better way to create a brilliant moment than to host the #SlumberPartyOfTheYear?

Real Job

Step 1: Invite your kid's five best friends over.
Step 2: Let them have unlimited soda, pizza, and ice cream.

HELPFUL HINTS! Make sure to have at least twelve hours of kids' DVDs ready since these kids will not be going to sleep tonight.

Fancy Job

Step 1: Invite your kid's five best friends over to your cabin.
Step 2: Let them camp out in the yard and watch movies projected against the wall of the cabin.

HELPFUL HINTS! Make sure you invite the parents for the weekend as well so you can drink some good scotch and have grown-up conversations about your first time playing spin the bottle.

Trust Fund

Step 1: Invite your kid's five best friends over to your Palm Springs compound.
Step 2: Have a weekend of guided hikes, golf, and swimming lessons.

HELPFUL HINTS! Make sure to create a weekend-long points challenge for standout performances in all the county club sports. The winner takes the jet home, losers fly commercial.

Play Dates for Business and Love

Congratulations! You now have a golden #BabyTicket to the secret society of parents! Forget about awkward icebreakers; now you have something in common with almost everyone between twenty-three and ninety-five years old. Your new connection will help you more than you ever dreamed with business and dating. I know it's tough to balance work, love, and family, but if you can manage to hang on to your #ChildlessFriends, your kid will double your network. Here's how to get some of the money back you're about to invest in your child. And if you're single, here's how to find other motivated single parents to date.

Real Job

Step 1: Host a Sunday BBQ after church and invite all your friends with kids.
Step 2: While you're cooking, your wife can work the crowd with all the new Tupperware options.

HELPFUL HINTS! Make sure you have a few side hustles to cover the costs of raising your kids.

Fancy Job

Step 1: Enjoy your post-divorce phase of dating much younger partners.
Step 2: Accept that you eventually need to date other grown-ups with kids.

HELPFUL HINTS! If you set up your dating app to your same age range, you can hit the same wave of other divorced parents and even date some people way out of your league who are new to the dating scene.

Trust Fund

Step 1: After your latest failed attempt at a merger, invite your chief business rival's family to take a trip with your family.
Step 2: Make sure your kids and their kids become best friends or, better yet, a couple, and let them sort out the merger.

HELPFUL HINTS! Make sure that you find something for the kids to do without you around so they can bond—after you've explained the importance of this damn merger.

Why You Should Not Hire a Hot Nanny

This one should seem obvious, but many a family has fallen into the trap of hiring a hot nanny. Even in the most loving and trusting families, there is a risk with inserting a third person into the mix. If that third person is young and beautiful, the risk grows exponentially. Unless you want jealousy to visit you in your most exhausted and vulnerable hours, here's why you should not hire a hot nanny.

Real Job

Step 1: You want your wife to feel pretty.
Step 2: Hire a babysitter that is less attractive than your wife.

HELPFUL HINTS! Another perk of an ugly nanny is that they're much less likely to fake being sick to go on a hot date and mess up *your* date night.

Fancy Job

Step 1: Have your assistant set up interviews with potential nannies.
Step 2: Let your wife pick the nanny.

HELPFUL HINTS! You basically just need to let your wife pick the nanny and manage the show, and you're good.

Trust Fund

Step 1: You were already forced to fire your last personal assistant.
Step 2: Your father-in-law is ninety years old and controls 18 percent of the shipping traffic between LA and China.

HELPFUL HINTS! You and your wife have a mutual understanding about the reality of lifelong monogamy, unlimited wealth, and power, but for god's sake don't be a cliché with the nanny.

Why You Should Hire a Hot Nanny

They say it takes a village to raise a child. The problem is that almost no one lives in a village anymore. Let's face it, villages have pretty limited food and entertainment options, and the potential for upward mobility sucks. It's probably more truthful to say that it takes the staff of a small business to raise a kid. One of those people on that staff will be a nanny. Here's why you should hire a hot nanny.

Real Job

Step 1: Parents should raise kids, not nannies.
Step 2: Call your babysitter a part-time nanny; it sounds fancier.

HELPFUL HINTS! It doesn't matter if your babysitter is hot as long as they show up on time and don't invite their boyfriend over when you're gone.

Fancy Job

Step 1: Have your assistant line up interviews of nannies for you and your wife.
Step 2: Interview all the nannies first and pick the most attractive for second-round interviews.

HELPFUL HINTS! Make a note to sympathize with your wife about the subtle discrimination that beautiful women face in the work world. Hire the hottest nanny.

Trust Fund

Step 1: You want only the best for your children...
Step 2: ...Including the nannies that will inevitably raise said children.

HELPFUL HINTS! Your nanny will be a teacher, parent, and life coach to your kids. If you want your kids to look up to their nanny, then make sure to hire an educated, funny, and beautiful one.

How to Fire Your Nanny

Breaking up is hard to do—especially when you know your kid will cry for days, and if they're old enough, write about how you are a terrible parent in their diary. There are usually two reasons why you have to fire a nanny. They might be terribly lazy and unreliable, or you or your partner might decide to quit work to actually raise your kids yourself.

Real Job

Step 1: Your nanny is really just an hourly babysitter.
Step 2: Cancel date night for the next twelve years and play Legos with the kids.

HELPFUL HINTS! Your mom pressed you to start a family for years, so let her have scheduled "Grandma time" to enjoy a night with your partner at your favorite bar each Friday.

Fancy Job

Step 1: Check with your attorney for a boilerplate severance and release agreement.
Step 2: Explain that the last pullback in the market really hit your budget and it's not their fault.

HELPFUL HINTS! Your husband just left a stressful six-figure job to raise the kids and run the household. You suspect he's really working on becoming a novelist and improving his golf game. If he can cook well and let you "travel for work," don't ask too many questions.

Trust Fund

Step 1: In your annual review with your accountant, you realize you have a nanny on payroll whom you thought you fired last year.
Step 2: Take them off payroll.

HELPFUL HINTS! Ask your personal assistant to schedule monthly performance reviews of your nannies and let her hire and fire them for you.

Teaching Your Teen to Invest and Bet

You want your kids to get ahead in life, and there are two ways to do that. The quick way is called betting (or day trading), and the slow way is called investing. Betting is where you win or lose a lot in a short amount of time. Betting is way more fun, but there's a reason that there are few independently wealthy bettors—also sometimes derided as gamblers. Investing is where you have a high degree of certainty of making a little bit of money but not much risk of losing said money. It's painfully boring, but you usually get rich in the end, and we all know that money equals happiness. You want your kids to be happy, right?

Real Job

Step 1: Wall Street is for suckers, and so are credit cards.
Step 2: Teach your kid to buy a home and pay it off.

HELPFUL HINTS! The secret is to convince your kids not to buy things they can't afford.

Fancy Job

Step 1: Teach your kids early to make more than they need and invest the balance.
Step 2: Cut your kids in on a value-add apartment deal early and make them paint all the units to get their cut of the deal.

HELPFUL HINTS! Nothing says happy birthday more than a ticket to a Robert Kiyosaki seminar!

Trust Fund

Step 1: Invent a dinnertime game called "Let's Create a Derivative" and play it every night.
Step 2: Get your teen a summer internship at the Goldman trading desk.

HELPFUL HINTS! If your kid gets their Series 7 license before they turn sixteen, they get to pick out their own BMW (or Tesla if they insist on keeping an office in Brooklyn).

Advanced Potty Training

There's an old saying that goes "Aim for the stars so even if you miss, you'll hit the moon." I've been shooting my bow and arrow at the stars for years, and all I've gotten is complaints from the neighbors. We all know that changing diapers is a drag, so the quicker you can teach your kid to aim and shoot successfully in the toilet, the quicker you can ditch the diapers. #AdvancedPottyTraining uses a mix of coaching, bribery, and encouragement, with just a dash of passive-aggressive shaming. The way my mom tells it, I was very food motivated and tricked out of my diapers and into big-boy pants with Hershey's Kisses every time I hit the target. Maybe that's why I still drink coffee in the bathroom and beer in the shower.

Real Job

Step 1: Explain to your kid that they can't have a BB gun if they can't hit the toilet.
Step 2: Get some superhero undies as a reward for motivation.

HELPFUL HINTS! Have a peeing competition, but don't cross streams!

Fancy Job

Step 1: Find the best daycare school in your neighborhood.
Step 2: Let the daycare school do the potty training.

HELPFUL HINTS! Make sure to get plenty of pics to celebrate this milestone on Instagram using your kid's personal #BabyHashtag.

Trust Fund

Step 1: One of your nannies has a master's degree in early childhood development.
Step 2: Remember which nanny has the master's and add potty training to their task list.

HELPFUL HINTS! Even if you're in Asia for the month, meeting with clients and vendors, you can schedule a Facetime session to give Junior some kudos for getting into their big-boy pants! After all, you did promise that you'd be present as a parent, didn't you?

Lasagna Week:
Introducing Your Baby to the World

There are only a couple times in life when you get people to make your meals and deliver them to your house. One of those times is when you have a brand-new baby to show off to the world. You spent nine months making and delivering a baby, so the least your friends can do is bring over a lasagna from Costco that they lovingly transferred to a Pyrex container so they can say it's from scratch. Phase one of baby tour week starts at home, so make sure to let your friends and family know what they can bring over. Phase two is when you take your new human out into the world while in a sleep-deprived delirious haze. Welcome to #LasagnaWeek.

Real Job

Step 1: Hit up the church phone tree with food and supply requests.
Step 2: Yes, beer counts as supplies.

HELPFUL HINTS! Practice setting up the folding stroller your sister-in-law gave you, because that thing is like a Rubik's cube!

Fancy Job

Step 1: Debut your kid's personal #BabyHashtag on social media and invite your friends over.
Step 2: Remind your friends that you are pro-paleo and anti-gluten and dairy.

HELPFUL HINTS! You both keep a strict, clean diet. A friend brings a lasagna anyway. Secretly binge on it in the kitchen after everyone is in bed.

Trust Fund

Step 1: Decide which house is best for introducing your baby to the world.
Step 2: Set up a destination baby week and ask friends and family to bring a small gift from their region.

HELPFUL HINTS! It's January, so obviously you pick the family compound in Palm Springs. Make sure your chef has everything for a locally sourced lasagna.

Winning Kindergarten

There are moments and milestones that define a successful life. The bigger your kid's goals and the more risks they take, the bigger a life they will have. You want your kid to have a great, big life that other people will envy on social media, right? The first step in the life of a winner is #WinningKindergarten. Here's how to make sure your kid doesn't have to repeat kindergarten (like me) and fall behind the pack.

Real Job

Step 1: Give your kid a Vince Lombardi-style pep talk on day one of kindergarten.
Step 2: If they learn the alphabet, they get to play Pop Warner football.

HELPFUL HINTS! If your kid loves sports, they will work to keep that GPA up so they don't get put on academic probation.

Fancy Job

Step 1: Enroll your kid into an aggressively academic pre-K program.
Step 2: Get a weekly fingerpainting tutor scheduled at least one year before kindergarten.

HELPFUL HINTS! Start an Etsy page to sell all those fingerpainted masterpieces to pay for the tutoring.

Trust Fund

Step 1: Success requires a fearless independence.
Step 2: Send your kid to a kindergarten boarding school.

HELPFUL HINTS! Make sure you pick a kindergarten program that guarantees your kid will be accepted to the best primary boarding school without you having to build a science lab or gym for the school.

How to Break Up
with Your Childless Friends

Remember when you were younger and your friends would invite you to a party on Friday night two hours before it started and everyone would show up? That's not your life anymore. Life now takes a shared online calendar and a host of babysitters, family help, nannies, teachers, daycare providers, and more. There's nothing more annoying than your childless friends who decide to work remotely in Buenos Aires for a couple months just because "it sounded fun!" Also, it gets embarrassing to turn down invitations to dinner parties and weekends at the coast because your babysitter cancels last minute. You'll be happier without all those out-of-touch #ChildlessFriends in your life, so here's how to break up with them.

Real Job

Step 1: You tell your friends you can't go to the bar after work.
Step 2: Try to ignore the looks of pity in their eyes.

HELPFUL HINTS! If you play your cards right, you can still get in a guys' weekend of fishing or hunting once or twice a year.

Fancy Job

Step 1: You tell your friends you can't go to the bar after work.
Step 2: Explain to everyone that family is your focus now.

HELPFUL HINTS! Convince your boss and wife that you need to take clients golfing more often, then invite your friends instead.

Trust Fund

Step 1: You tell your friends you can't go to the bar after work.
Step 2: You remember that you own the company and meet them for lunch instead.

HELPFUL HINTS! Your therapist will help you accept that you can't take the jet to St. Barts after a good week in the market for a Thursday-through-Sunday bender with your friends anymore.

How to Make New Friends When You Lose All Your Single Friends

Now that you've broken up with your #ChildlessFriends, or they've simply stopped inviting you to their parties, it's time to find new friends—friends that understand that you can't leave the house and need a couple weeks to plan a night on the town that will end promptly at 11:00 p.m. While this might sound dire, there is an upside. As you go through the pregnancy and birth process, your friend group will expand to include #ParentFriends. Also, based on your evangelical espousing of the joys of parenting, some of your childless friends will decide to have kids too.

Real Job

Step 1: Sign up for a parenting class at your church.
Step 2: Have a potluck baby shower with the whole group of new and expecting parents.

HELPFUL HINTS! Set up a weekly get-together so you don't lose your mind. Sunday afternoon is a good time, especially during football season.

Fancy Job

Step 1: Sign up for baby yoga, Lamaze classes, and baby boot camp.
Step 2: Exchange info with the whole group of new and expecting parents.

HELPFUL HINTS! Sponsor the cost of a couple babysitters for all your new friends so you can go to brunch together, then write it off as a business meeting.

Trust Fund

Step 1: Take six months off to bond with your new baby and two nannies at the family retreat compound.
Step 2: Invite your friends with kids to join you and use one of the guest houses for a week.

HELPFUL HINTS! Make sure you invite some friends with a couple years of parenting experience to learn how to balance your new kids and nannies while maintaining as much of your former lifestyle as possible.

How to Keep Having Sex

Sex feels good. If you do sex well, it feels good for you *and* your partner. Sex is also a great way to make up and smooth out the rough edges when you say or do something stupid. Why, then, is it so hard to keep having sex? To #KeepHavingSex, you need to have energy and feel sexy. Babies are bad for both of those things. The secret is to make time for yourself and each other and find a place where you won't get interrupted for at least ten minutes a couple days a week.

Real Job

Step 1: Embrace his new dad bod.
Step 2: Embrace her new mom bod.

HELPFUL HINTS! If either of you is exhausted, just try for a lying-down-on-your-sides, doggie-style position. You can almost fall asleep and still make it happen.

Fancy Job

Step 1: Add workout goals to your shared calendar.
Step 2: Use sex as a reward for your weight and exercise goals.

HELPFUL HINTS! Add an extra hour per day with your childcare helper to run a quick 5k in the park together and have sex against the wall in the steam shower when you're done.

Trust Fund

Step 1: You both know rest is important.
Step 2: Set up the baby's room near the nanny's quarters in the opposite
wing of the house.

HELPFUL HINTS! Make love with the rising sun and take a quick nap before you join the rest of the household for brunch and a photo op with the family.

If You Stop Crying, I'll Buy You a Pony: How to Lie to Your Kids

Probably the most underrated skill you're going to need as a parent is lying. Kids are total suckers until they hit about nine years old. Until then, you are literally God, and what you say goes, period. A good friend used to tell me that whenever his daughter would cry, he would tell her that if she stopped crying, he would buy her a pony. That's an excellent lie on the list of top #ParentLies. You're also going to need to lie about Santa Claus, the Easter bunny, and the tooth fairy. Lying is fun when your kids believe all of it. The only downside is that in sixty years when your kids put you in a home, they're going to start lying to you, and then you'll be the sucker.

Real Job

Step 1: Tell the kids that you're just resting your eyelids when you nap on the couch and that you can still hear everything.
Step 2: Enjoy a blissful moment of quiet.

HELPFUL HINTS! Try to lie about things your kids can't disprove, like Santa, for as long as possible.

Fancy Job

Step 1: Refer to the personality profile test your kids do each year to remember their biggest fears.
Step 2: Use those deep-rooted fears, along with carefully crafted #ParentLies, to get what you want.

HELPFUL HINTS! Check out the Myers-Briggs or DISC test; these are also great for spouses.

Trust Fund

Step 1: Tell your kids you're very busy with a new business venture.
Step 2: Go skiing in the Alps.

HELPFUL HINTS! I'm just kidding. You have a day nanny and a night nanny for a reason. The kids get to go skiing in the Alps this year. But if they don't make the dean's list next semester, they're out of the family trust.

Tips for Winning Couple's Therapy

We all have disagreements, and it can be difficult to get along sometimes. Add to that the stress of being a parent, and the nerves can get frayed more easily—and when nerves get frayed, the claws come out. You love your spouse and you couldn't live without them, but that doesn't mean you have to give up and just roll over. When you get to the point that you need therapy, here's how to make sure you #WinCouplesTherapy.

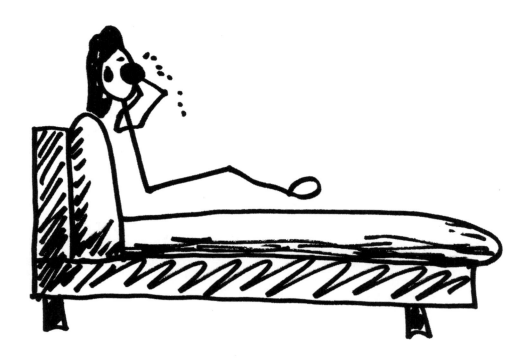

Real Job

Step 1: You don't have a therapist, so your pastor offers to help.
Step 2: Talk about Jesus a lot; pastors love that stuff. Then just say you're sorry.

HELPFUL HINTS! If you say you're sorry, you can stop going to therapy, and that counts as a win.

Fancy Job

Step 1: Mutually pick a therapist that comes from a philosophical school you agree on.
Step 2: Cry in front of the therapist when you talk about love. Your wife has never seen you cry, so this will be disarming.

HELPFUL HINTS! Make sure that you have insurance that covers this stuff. It can really add up if you're paying out of pocket.

Trust Fund

Step 1: Narrow the field to APA-award recipients with at least one TED talk.
Step 2: Meet with the therapist alone first to explain the concept of performance bonuses and your goals in this relationship. Use your special wink if things start to go south during a session.

HELPFUL HINTS! You can avoid paying for this silly exercise simply by offering to refer some of your investors to the therapist after you credit her with saving your marriage.

Teaching Your Teen to Drink

Your kids are going to drink. Unless you teach them proper drinking techniques, they're going to suck at drinking. When you suck at drinking, you get in trouble when you drink. You want your kids to be better than the drunk teen version of you who puked in the sink at Susie's big party, right? It's time for #DrinkingLessons.

Real Job

Step 1: Take your kid camping.
Step 2: See who can drink the most light beer, then ask 'em to tie a hook to a fishing line and fail so they know why they can't drive drunk.

HELPFUL HINTS! If they stick the hook in their finger, the lesson will last longer.

Fancy Job

Step 1: Explain the fine line between social drinking and problem drinking.
Step 2: Teach your kid about their limit based on their body weight and metabolism, then have your teen practice with a breathalyzer.

HELPFUL HINTS! There's nothing more embarrassing than when your kid mixes up vodka and gin and screws up a perfectly good martini, so make sure they know the difference.

Trust Fund

Step 1: Your favorite kid developed a preference for pinots over cabernets before high school.
Step 2: Teach your kid to detect the differences between different regions and AVAs (American Viticultural Areas) in their wine.

HELPFUL HINTS! You have a driver, so you're not worried about DUIs, but for god's sake, those kids better not end up on *Page Six* when you're trying to close your second round of funding from Saudi investors.

How to Hide from the Kids

Kids are both the best and worst thing that will ever happen to you. Regardless of your state of mind or the state of your relationship with your kids, sometimes you just want to hide and enjoy the silence. Don't feel guilty. Here's how to #HideFromTheKids.

Real Job

Step 1: Tell your wife you're getting a second job.
Step 2: Only show up a couple hours a week; go fishing the rest of the time.

HELPFUL HINTS! Sales jobs are perfect since you only get paid if you close a deal and no one keeps a time sheet.

Fancy Job

Step 1: Ask the CEO to send you overseas to China more often.
Step 2: Learn Chinese, close a huge acquisition, and buy a beach house.

HELPFUL HINTS! Having two houses gives you twice the opportunity to hide from your kids.

Trust Fund

Step 1: Get two nannies.
Step 2: Find an excellent Montessori boarding school, primary boarding school, and prep boarding school.

HELPFUL HINTS! No one will question that your choice of boarding schools is designed to give your children the best education possible. If a friend questions your choice of schools, just remind them that this is how you went through school, and you're fine. Just fine!

How to Minimize Cock-Blocking

I t's hard to maintain the energy to keep having sex. There's nothing worse than when the stars align and you're both in the mood and then someone starts crying or barges into the bedroom. Just when you think there's no one left to screw up your sex life, you add kids to the mix and the whole thing starts over again. You're not going to bat a thousand, but here's how to #MinimizeCockBlocking.

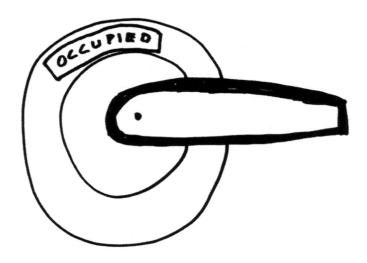

Real Job

Step 1: Drop the kids at your mom's house for date night.
Step 2: Drive off together into the woods to sneak in a quickie.

HELPFUL HINTS! Make sure to have the quickie before dinner. You don't want to cockblock yourself with indigestion.

Fancy Job

Step 1: Plan a couple of regional work trips at nice resorts.
Step 2: Take your partner with you on the work trip.

HELPFUL HINTS! Book your meetings in the middle of the day so you can make love in the morning and at night with no stress.

Trust Fund

Step 1: Emotional boundaries are important for raising independent kids.
Step 2: Take plenty of trips without the kids.

HELPFUL HINTS! It's tough being a parent before boarding school starts, so make sure to plan plenty of trips as a couple. It seems like a waste to bring Junior to Paris when he can't appreciate the wine and cheese yet.

How to Sell the Dad Bod Thing

I'm pretty sure you've heard of the #DadBod phenomenon by now, but if not, here's the deal: gone is the Adonis or Abercrombie & Fitch model ideal of the male physique, and in is the slightly doughy and totally nonthreatening soft male body known as a #DadBod. This new ideal is why I only work out once a week. While I was once worried it was a fad, it turns out, ladies—even very fit, athletic ladies—are totally into this thing. Here's how to find out if your baby momma is into the soft serve, or maybe a bit less so, and still sell it anyway.

Real Job

Step 1: You don't need to go to the gym since you actually work for a living.
Step 2: Drink light beer.

HELPFUL HINTS! Clean your hands. Ladies like clean hands.

Fancy Job

Step 1: Take a baking class and make wonderful treats.
Step 2: Start using a standing desk.

HELPFUL HINTS! Sitting is the new smoking. Remind your wife that you'll never make partner if you're at the gym every day.

Trust Fund

Step 1: Remind yourself and your wife that you're not on the Harvard rugby team anymore.
Step 2: Then remember that Yves Saint Laurent doesn't make 2XL suits.
Step 3: Secretly work out to maintain your physique.

HELPFUL HINTS! If you only eat twice a day and drink vodka and sodas, you can limit workouts to three times a week.

How to Make a Baby

This chapter is my personal favorite. I've never made a baby, but I've done 90 percent of the necessary steps a couple thousand times and enjoyed it every time. While it might seem like it's obvious how to make a baby, people are waiting longer and longer into life to start families these days. You might have to have sex with your spouse more than once to make it happen, but don't despair, because babies are in your future! Here's #HowToMakeABaby.

Real Job

Step 1: Take your lady out dancing and make sure there are at least a couple slow songs.
Step 2: Have sex on the kitchen counter after the concert.

HELPFUL HINTS! Don't get too drunk—you have to finish to make a baby.

Fancy Job

Step 1: Stress is a baby-making no-no, so book a trip to an all-inclusive tropical locale.
Step 2: Enjoy a week of sunny beaches, couples' yoga, and lovemaking with the windows of your beach bungalow open to the sound of the waves crashing on the reef.

HELPFUL HINTS! Turn off your phone and don't read the news.

Trust Fund

Step 1: Hire a captain to sail your grandfather's yacht from Boston to Bermuda.
Step 2: Drink martinis and make love the entire trip.

HELPFUL HINTS! Take breaks in your lovemaking to work on your tans. You don't want to come back from the islands without a nice glow.

Change Your Own Diaper!

Here now is my best advice for you on your parenting journey: An easy life is not the best life. If you want to make your dreams come true, you've got to work and fight for what you want. The only person responsible for your success is you. And no matter how great a parent you are, the only person responsible for your kid's success as an adult is them. What better way to teach your kids self-reliance than to start early? Money doesn't grow on trees, and diapers don't change themselves, so you better learn to change your own diaper. #ChangeYourOwnDiaper!

Real Job

Step 1: Your kid dreams of owning a truck by their sixteenth birthday.
Step 2: Get them a 1978 Chevy long-bed rolling chassis and Haynes repair manual.

HELPFUL HINTS! Have fun teaching them how to rebuild a rig, but don't do it for them.

Fancy Job

Step 1: Your kid dreams of writing a book.
Step 2: Get your aspiring writer *On Writing* by Stephen King and *Consider This* by Chuck Palahniuk.
Step 3: Schedule writing every day, and publish, publish, publish.

HELPFUL HINTS! Hire an up-and-coming editor to work on your kid's selection of short stories. Publish it on Amazon for their birthday.

Trust Fund

Step 1: Your kid dreams of starting a company that is even better than yours.
Step 2: Get them a series of summer internships at startups beginning in sixth grade.

HELPFUL HINTS! Invest in your kid's startups early. If they fail, your company still succeeds, and if they disrupt you, you'll already be a majority shareholder. Win-win!

How to Accept
All the Terrible Decisions
Your Kid Will Make in College

Kids do the darndest things. When they are young, the mistakes are cute and all about learning. As kids get older, their terrible decisions tend to come with bigger consequences and therefore even more familial disappointment. If you thought high school was bad, just wait until they get to college. At this point you've done your best to help your kids make it on their own. Here's how to accept all the #TerribleCollegeDecisions they're going to make.

Real Job

Step 1: Your kid will get a full sleeve tattoo in college.
Step 2: If you don't mention it, you can pretend it's not real.

HELPFUL HINTS! Buy your kid long-sleeved shirts for Christmas to help cover it up.

Fancy Job

Step 1: Your kid gets engaged to their crazy college sweetheart.
Step 2: Plan a trip to meet the parents.

HELPFUL HINTS! Convince your kid that a prenup is the best way to make sure their partner is in it for the right reasons.

Trust Fund

Step 1: Your kid decides to study poetry in college.
Step 2: Pay for it anyway; pretend you're excited.

HELPFUL HINTS! Remind yourself that philosophy was your third-favorite course when you went to college and that it helps to look well rounded when working with your European companies.

Winning Empty Nesting, Part One: What to Talk about When You Can't Talk about the Kids

You spent twenty-five glorious years raising your kids, and now you're finally going to get your old life back. The problem is that neither of you can remember what your old life was like before the kids. No more soccer camps and daily practices. No more meetings with the school counselor and parent-teacher nights. It's like you've been working two full-time jobs the last two decades and you just got to retire from one of them. To help you recapture what life was like when you were cool, here's a guide to #WinningEmptyNesting.

Real Job

Step 1: You come home from work.
Step 2: It's beautifully quiet.

HELPFUL HINTS! Have a beer together on the front porch and plan a road trip to somewhere you actually want to go.

Fancy Job

Step 1: You've been preparing for the emotional crisis of not being active parents.
Step 2: It happens anyway.

HELPFUL HINTS! Recreate a European cycling trip you took together before you had kids and reconnect as a couple.

Trust Fund

Step 1: Take the jet to St. Barts with just the two of you.
Step 2: Drink champagne and make love in the back of the jet like you used to do before you had kids.

HELPFUL HINTS! Make sure to have a half case of champagne and some Viagra. The flight from NYC always takes longer than you think.

Winning Empty Nesting, Part Two: Sports Cars and Sex in the Kitchen

The best part of empty nesting is all the time and money you get back, especially once the kids are out of college and you're not burning $50,000 a year on a degree that will likely lead to a career as a barista. There is a downside, though, to all that extra time and money: How, oh how, will you spend it?

Real Job

Step 1: Buy a boat.
Step 2: Go fishing every day.

HELPFUL HINTS! Find a great deal on a used "midlife" Chrysler convertible for the missus.

Fancy Job

Step 1: Buy a Porsche.
Step 2: Have spontaneous sex on the kitchen counter, overcooked pasta
      be damned.

HELPFUL HINTS! You can finally visit Palm Springs outside of spring break and spend the savings on better golf courses.

Trust Fund

Step 1: Save $200,000 a year on your kid's tuition at NYU and loft in Soho.
Step 2: Your kid asks for $1 million to start a B Corp in Brooklyn. Ugh.

HELPFUL HINTS! Your CFO explains that millennials love to support B Corps, and they can still turn a healthy profit. Rebrand one of your failing subsidiary companies as a B Corp and revel in the turnaround.

About the Author

Nick Krautter knows very little about actually raising kids other than what he hears from his friends who insist on telling him that parenting is amazing. He fills the childless void in his life with an unending list of hobbies, businesses, spontaneous trips, golf, hot dates, and projects. This book started as a joke at a baby shower, and as long as it makes Nick and his friends with kids laugh, he'll keep writing.

HELPFUL HINTS! Make sure to buy a copy of this book for anyone you know who is pregnant, has kids, or was a kid at some point in their life.

Made in USA - Crawfordsville, IN
24636_9780996814645
05.23.2023 1845